My Gratitude Journal

name: ....

This week ....

TODAY ....   **I AM GRATEFUL FOR:**

1. ....
2. ....
3. ....

TODAY ....   **I AM GRATEFUL FOR:**

1. ....
2. ....
3. ....

TODAY ....   **I AM GRATEFUL FOR:**

1. ....
2. ....
3. ....

TODAY .... I AM GRATEFUL FOR:

1. ....

2. ....

3. ....

TODAY .... I AM GRATEFUL FOR:

1. ....

2. ....

3. ....

TODAY .... I AM GRATEFUL FOR:

1. ....

2. ....

3. ....

TODAY .... I AM GRATEFUL FOR:

1. ....

2. ....

3. ....

This week ....

TODAY ....   I AM GRATEFUL FOR:

1. ....
2. ....
3. ....

TODAY ....   I AM GRATEFUL FOR:

1. ....
2. ....
3. ....

TODAY ....   I AM GRATEFUL FOR:

1. ....
2. ....
3. ....

TODY .... I AM GRATEFUL FOR:

1. ....
2. ....
3. ....

TODAY .... I AM GRATEFUL FOR:

1. ....
2. ....
3. ....

TODAY .... I AM GRATEFUL FOR:

1. ....
2. ....
3. ....

TODAY .... I AM GRATEFUL FOR:

1. ....
2. ....
3. ....

This week ....

TODAY ....   I AM GRATEFUL FOR:

1. ....
2. ....
3. ....

TODAY ....   I AM GRATEFUL FOR:

1. ....
2. ....
3. ....

TODAY ....   I AM GRATEFUL FOR:

1. ....
2. ....
3. ....

TODY .... I AM GRATEFUL FOR:

1. ....

2. ....

3. ....

TODAY .... I AM GRATEFUL FOR:

1. ....

2. ....

3. ....

TODAY .... I AM GRATEFUL FOR:

1. ....

2. ....

3. ....

TODAY .... I AM GRATEFUL FOR:

1. ....

2. ....

3. ....

This week ....

TODAY ....   I AM GRATEFUL FOR:

1. ....
2. ....
3. ....

TODAY ....   I AM GRATEFUL FOR:

1. ....
2. ....
3. ....

TODAY ....   I AM GRATEFUL FOR:

1. ....
2. ....
3. ....

TODAY .... I AM GRATEFUL FOR:

1. ....

2. ....

3. ....

TODAY .... I AM GRATEFUL FOR:

1. ....

2. ....

3. ....

TODAY .... I AM GRATEFUL FOR:

1. ....

2. ....

3. ....

TODAY .... I AM GRATEFUL FOR:

1. ....

2. ....

3. ....

This week ....

TODAY .... I AM GRATEFUL FOR:

1. ....

2. ....

3. ....

TODAY .... I AM GRATEFUL FOR:

1. ....

2. ....

3. ....

TODAY .... I AM GRATEFUL FOR:

1. ....

2. ....

3. ....

TODAY .... I AM GRATEFUL FOR:

1. ....

2. ....

3. ....

TODAY .... I AM GRATEFUL FOR:

1. ....

2. ....

3. ....

TODAY .... I AM GRATEFUL FOR:

1. ....

2. ....

3. ....

TODAY .... I AM GRATEFUL FOR:

1. ....

2. ....

3. ....

This week ....

TODAY ....   I AM GRATEFUL FOR:

1. ....

2. ....

3. ....

TODAY ....   I AM GRATEFUL FOR:

1. ....

2. ....

3. ....

TODAY ....   I AM GRATEFUL FOR:

1. ....

2. ....

3. ....

TODAY .... I AM GRATEFUL FOR:

1. ....

2. ....

3. ....

TODAY .... I AM GRATEFUL FOR:

1. ....

2. ....

3. ....

TODAY .... I AM GRATEFUL FOR:

1. ....

2. ....

3. ....

TODAY .... I AM GRATEFUL FOR:

1. ....

2. ....

3. ....

This week ....

TODO .... I AM GRATEFUL FOR:

1. ....

2. ....

3. ....

TODAY .... I AM GRATEFUL FOR:

1. ....

2. ....

3. ....

TODAY .... I AM GRATEFUL FOR:

1. ....

2. ....

3. ....

TODY .... I AM GRATEFUL FOR:

1. ....

2. ....

3. ....

TODAY .... I AM GRATEFUL FOR:

1. ....

2. ....

3. ....

TODAY .... I AM GRATEFUL FOR:

1. ....

2. ....

3. ....

TODAY .... I AM GRATEFUL FOR:

1. ....

2. ....

3. ....

This week ....

TODAY ....   I AM GRATEFUL FOR:

1. ....

2. ....

3. ....

TODAY ....   I AM GRATEFUL FOR:

1. ....

2. ....

3. ....

TODAY ....   I AM GRATEFUL FOR:

1. ....

2. ....

3. ....

TODAY .... I AM GRATEFUL FOR:

1. ....
2. ....
3. ....

TODAY .... I AM GRATEFUL FOR:

1. ....
2. ....
3. ....

TODAY .... I AM GRATEFUL FOR:

1. ....
2. ....
3. ....

TODAY .... I AM GRATEFUL FOR:

1. ....
2. ....
3. ....

This week ....

TODAY .... I AM GRATEFUL FOR:

1. ....

2. ....

3. ....

TODAY .... I AM GRATEFUL FOR:

1. ....

2. ....

3. ....

TODAY .... I AM GRATEFUL FOR:

1. ....

2. ....

3. ....

TODAY .... I AM GRATEFUL FOR:

1. ....

2. ....

3. ....

TODAY .... I AM GRATEFUL FOR:

1. ....

2. ....

3. ....

TODAY .... I AM GRATEFUL FOR:

1. ....

2. ....

3. ....

TODAY .... I AM GRATEFUL FOR:

1. ....

2. ....

3. ....

This week ....

TODAY ....   I AM GRATEFUL FOR:

1. ....
2. ....
3. ....

TODAY ....   I AM GRATEFUL FOR:

1. ....
2. ....
3. ....

TODAY ....   I AM GRATEFUL FOR:

1. ....
2. ....
3. ....

TODAY .... I AM GRATEFUL FOR:

1. ....

2. ....

3. ....

TODAY .... I AM GRATEFUL FOR:

1. ....

2. ....

3. ....

TODAY .... I AM GRATEFUL FOR:

1. ....

2. ....

3. ....

TODAY .... I AM GRATEFUL FOR:

1. ....

2. ....

3. ....

This week ....

TODAY ....   I AM GRATEFUL FOR:

1. ....

2. ....

3. ....

TODAY ....   I AM GRATEFUL FOR:

1. ....

2. ....

3. ....

TODAY ....   I AM GRATEFUL FOR:

1. ....

2. ....

3. ....

TODAY .... I AM GRATEFUL FOR:

1. ....

2. ....

3. ....

TODAY .... I AM GRATEFUL FOR:

1. ....

2. ....

3. ....

TODAY .... I AM GRATEFUL FOR:

1. ....

2. ....

3. ....

TODAY .... I AM GRATEFUL FOR:

1. ....

2. ....

3. ....

This week ....

TODAY .... I AM GRATEFUL FOR:

1. ....

2. ....

3. ....

TODAY .... I AM GRATEFUL FOR:

1. ....

2. ....

3. ....

TODAY .... I AM GRATEFUL FOR:

1. ....

2. ....

3. ....

TODAY .... I AM GRATEFUL FOR:

1. ....

2. ....

3. ....

TODAY .... I AM GRATEFUL FOR:

1. ....

2. ....

3. ....

TODAY .... I AM GRATEFUL FOR:

1. ....

2. ....

3. ....

TODAY .... I AM GRATEFUL FOR:

1. ....

2. ....

3. ....

This week ....

TODAY ....   I AM GRATEFUL FOR:

1. ....

2. ....

3. ....

TODAY ....   I AM GRATEFUL FOR:

1. ....

2. ....

3. ....

TODAY ....   I AM GRATEFUL FOR:

1. ....

2. ....

3. ....

TODAY .... I AM GRATEFUL FOR:

1. ....

2. ....

3. ....

TODAY .... I AM GRATEFUL FOR:

1. ....

2. ....

3. ....

TODAY .... I AM GRATEFUL FOR:

1. ....

2. ....

3. ....

TODAY .... I AM GRATEFUL FOR:

1. ....

2. ....

3. ....

This week ....

TODAY ....   I AM GRATEFUL FOR:

1. ....

2. ....

3. ....

TODAY ....   I AM GRATEFUL FOR:

1. ....

2. ....

3. ....

TODAY ....   I AM GRATEFUL FOR:

1. ....

2. ....

3. ....

TODAY .... I AM GRATEFUL FOR:

1. ....

2. ....

3. ....

TODAY .... I AM GRATEFUL FOR:

1. ....

2. ....

3. ....

TODAY .... I AM GRATEFUL FOR:

1. ....

2. ....

3. ....

TODAY .... I AM GRATEFUL FOR:

1. ....

2. ....

3. ....

This week ....

TODAY ....   I AM GRATEFUL FOR:

1. ....

2. ....

3. ....

TODAY ....   I AM GRATEFUL FOR:

1. ....

2. ....

3. ....

TODAY ....   I AM GRATEFUL FOR:

1. ....

2. ....

3. ....

TODAY .... I AM GRATEFUL FOR:

1. ....

2. ....

3. ....

TODAY .... I AM GRATEFUL FOR:

1. ....

2. ....

3. ....

TODAY .... I AM GRATEFUL FOR:

1. ....

2. ....

3. ....

TODAY .... I AM GRATEFUL FOR:

1. ....

2. ....

3. ....

This week ....

TODAY ....   I AM GRATEFUL FOR:

1. ....

2. ....

3. ....

TODAY ....   I AM GRATEFUL FOR:

1. ....

2. ....

3. ....

TODAY ....   I AM GRATEFUL FOR:

1. ....

2. ....

3. ....

TODAY .... I AM GRATEFUL FOR:

1. ....

2. ....

3. ....

TODAY .... I AM GRATEFUL FOR:

1. ....

2. ....

3. ....

TODAY .... I AM GRATEFUL FOR:

1. ....

2. ....

3. ....

TODAY .... I AM GRATEFUL FOR:

1. ....

2. ....

3. ....

This week ....

TODAY ....   I AM GRATEFUL FOR:

1. ....

2. ....

3. ....

TODAY ....   I AM GRATEFUL FOR:

1. ....

2. ....

3. ....

TODAY ....   I AM GRATEFUL FOR:

1. ....

2. ....

3. ....

TODAY .... I AM GRATEFUL FOR:

1. ....

2. ....

3. ....

TODAY .... I AM GRATEFUL FOR:

1. ....

2. ....

3. ....

TODAY .... I AM GRATEFUL FOR:

1. ....

2. ....

3. ....

TODAY .... I AM GRATEFUL FOR:

1. ....

2. ....

3. ....

This week ....

TODAY ....   I AM GRATEFUL FOR:

1. ....

2. ....

3. ....

TODAY ....   I AM GRATEFUL FOR:

1. ....

2. ....

3. ....

TODAY ....   I AM GRATEFUL FOR:

1. ....

2. ....

3. ....

TODAY .... I AM GRATEFUL FOR:

1. ....

2. ....

3. ....

TODAY .... I AM GRATEFUL FOR:

1. ....

2. ....

3. ....

TODAY .... I AM GRATEFUL FOR:

1. ....

2. ....

3. ....

TODAY .... I AM GRATEFUL FOR:

1. ....

2. ....

3. ....

This week ....

TODAY ....   I AM GRATEFUL FOR:

1. ....

2. ....

3. ....

TODAY ....   I AM GRATEFUL FOR:

1. ....

2. ....

3. ....

TODAY ....   I AM GRATEFUL FOR:

1. ....

2. ....

3. ....

TODAY .... I AM GRATEFUL FOR:

1. ....

2. ....

3. ....

TODAY .... I AM GRATEFUL FOR:

1. ....

2. ....

3. ....

TODAY .... I AM GRATEFUL FOR:

1. ....

2. ....

3. ....

TODAY .... I AM GRATEFUL FOR:

1. ....

2. ....

3. ....

This week ....

TODAY ....   I AM GRATEFUL FOR:

1. ....

2. ....

3. ....

TODAY ....   I AM GRATEFUL FOR:

1. ....

2. ....

3. ....

TODAY ....   I AM GRATEFUL FOR:

1. ....

2. ....

3. ....

TODAY .... I AM GRATEFUL FOR:

1. ....

2. ....

3. ....

TODAY .... I AM GRATEFUL FOR:

1. ....

2. ....

3. ....

TODAY .... I AM GRATEFUL FOR:

1. ....

2. ....

3. ....

TODAY .... I AM GRATEFUL FOR:

1. ....

2. ....

3. ....

This week ....

TODAY ....   I AM GRATEFUL FOR:

1. ....

2. ....

3. ....

TODAY ....   I AM GRATEFUL FOR:

1. ....

2. ....

3. ....

TODAY ....   I AM GRATEFUL FOR:

1. ....

2. ....

3. ....

TODAY .... I AM GRATEFUL FOR:

1. ....

2. ....

3. ....

TODAY .... I AM GRATEFUL FOR:

1. ....

2. ....

3. ....

TODAY .... I AM GRATEFUL FOR:

1. ....

2. ....

3. ....

TODAY .... I AM GRATEFUL FOR:

1. ....

2. ....

3. ....

This week ....

TODAY .... I AM GRATEFUL FOR:

1. ....

2. ....

3. ....

TODAY .... I AM GRATEFUL FOR:

1. ....

2. ....

3. ....

TODAY .... I AM GRATEFUL FOR:

1. ....

2. ....

3. ....

TODAY .... I AM GRATEFUL FOR:

1. ....
2. ....
3. ....

TODAY .... I AM GRATEFUL FOR:

1. ....
2. ....
3. ....

TODAY .... I AM GRATEFUL FOR:

1. ....
2. ....
3. ....

TODAY .... I AM GRATEFUL FOR:

1. ....
2. ....
3. ....

This week ....

TODAY ....   I AM GRATEFUL FOR:

1. ....

2. ....

3. ....

TODAY ....   I AM GRATEFUL FOR:

1. ....

2. ....

3. ....

TODAY ....   I AM GRATEFUL FOR:

1. ....

2. ....

3. ....

TODAY .... I AM GRATEFUL FOR:

1. ....

2. ....

3. ....

TODAY .... I AM GRATEFUL FOR:

1. ....

2. ....

3. ....

TODAY .... I AM GRATEFUL FOR:

1. ....

2. ....

3. ....

TODAY .... I AM GRATEFUL FOR:

1. ....

2. ....

3. ....

This week ....

TODAY ....   I AM GRATEFUL FOR:

1. ....

2. ....

3. ....

TODAY ....   I AM GRATEFUL FOR:

1. ....

2. ....

3. ....

TODAY ....   I AM GRATEFUL FOR:

1. ....

2. ....

3. ....

TODAY .... I AM GRATEFUL FOR:

1. ....

2. ....

3. ....

TODAY .... I AM GRATEFUL FOR:

1. ....

2. ....

3. ....

TODAY .... I AM GRATEFUL FOR:

1. ....

2. ....

3. ....

TODAY .... I AM GRATEFUL FOR:

1. ....

2. ....

3. ....

This week ....

TODAY ....   I AM GRATEFUL FOR:

1. ....

2. ....

3. ....

TODAY ....   I AM GRATEFUL FOR:

1. ....

2. ....

3. ....

TODAY ....   I AM GRATEFUL FOR:

1. ....

2. ....

3. ....

TODAY .... I AM GRATEFUL FOR:

1. ....

2. ....

3. ....

TODAY .... I AM GRATEFUL FOR:

1. ....

2. ....

3. ....

TODAY .... I AM GRATEFUL FOR:

1. ....

2. ....

3. ....

TODAY .... I AM GRATEFUL FOR:

1. ....

2. ....

3. ....

This week ....

TODAY ....   I AM GRATEFUL FOR:

1. ....
2. ....
3. ....

TODAY ....   I AM GRATEFUL FOR:

1. ....
2. ....
3. ....

TODAY ....   I AM GRATEFUL FOR:

1. ....
2. ....
3. ....

TODAY .... I AM GRATEFUL FOR:

1. ....

2. ....

3. ....

TODAY .... I AM GRATEFUL FOR:

1. ....

2. ....

3. ....

TODAY .... I AM GRATEFUL FOR:

1. ....

2. ....

3. ....

TODAY .... I AM GRATEFUL FOR:

1. ....

2. ....

3. ....

This week ....

TODAY ....   I AM GRATEFUL FOR:

1. ....
2. ....
3. ....

TODAY ....   I AM GRATEFUL FOR:

1. ....
2. ....
3. ....

TODAY ....   I AM GRATEFUL FOR:

1. ....
2. ....
3. ....

TODAY .... I AM GRATEFUL FOR:

1. ....

2. ....

3. ....

TODAY .... I AM GRATEFUL FOR:

1. ....

2. ....

3. ....

TODAY .... I AM GRATEFUL FOR:

1. ....

2. ....

3. ....

TODAY .... I AM GRATEFUL FOR:

1. ....

2. ....

3. ....

This week ....

TODAY ....   I AM GRATEFUL FOR:

1. ....
2. ....
3. ....

TODAY ....   I AM GRATEFUL FOR:

1. ....
2. ....
3. ....

TODAY ....   I AM GRATEFUL FOR:

1. ....
2. ....
3. ....

TODAY .... I AM GRATEFUL FOR:

1. ....

2. ....

3. ....

TODAY .... I AM GRATEFUL FOR:

1. ....

2. ....

3. ....

TODAY .... I AM GRATEFUL FOR:

1. ....

2. ....

3. ....

TODAY .... I AM GRATEFUL FOR:

1. ....

2. ....

3. ....

This week ....

TODAY ....   I AM GRATEFUL FOR:
1. ....
2. ....
3. ....

TODAY ....   I AM GRATEFUL FOR:
1. ....
2. ....
3. ....

TODAY ....   I AM GRATEFUL FOR:
1. ....
2. ....
3. ....

TODAY .... I AM GRATEFUL FOR:

1. ....

2. ....

3. ....

TODAY .... I AM GRATEFUL FOR:

1. ....

2. ....

3. ....

TODAY .... I AM GRATEFUL FOR:

1. ....

2. ....

3. ....

TODAY .... I AM GRATEFUL FOR:

1. ....

2. ....

3. ....

This week ....

TODAY ....   I AM GRATEFUL FOR:

1. ....

2. ....

3. ....

TODAY ....   I AM GRATEFUL FOR:

1. ....

2. ....

3. ....

TODAY ....   I AM GRATEFUL FOR:

1. ....

2. ....

3. ....

TODAY .... I AM GRATEFUL FOR:

1. ....

2. ....

3. ....

TODAY .... I AM GRATEFUL FOR:

1. ....

2. ....

3. ....

TODAY .... I AM GRATEFUL FOR:

1. ....

2. ....

3. ....

TODAY .... I AM GRATEFUL FOR:

1. ....

2. ....

3. ....

This week ....

TODAY ....   I AM GRATEFUL FOR:

1. ....

2. ....

3. ....

TODAY ....   I AM GRATEFUL FOR:

1. ....

2. ....

3. ....

TODAY ....   I AM GRATEFUL FOR:

1. ....

2. ....

3. ....

TODAY .... I AM GRATEFUL FOR:

1. ....
2. ....
3. ....

TODAY .... I AM GRATEFUL FOR:

1. ....
2. ....
3. ....

TODAY .... I AM GRATEFUL FOR:

1. ....
2. ....
3. ....

TODAY .... I AM GRATEFUL FOR:

1. ....
2. ....
3. ....

This week ....

TODAY ....   I AM GRATEFUL FOR:

1. ....

2. ....

3. ....

TODAY ....   I AM GRATEFUL FOR:

1. ....

2. ....

3. ....

TODAY ....   I AM GRATEFUL FOR:

1. ....

2. ....

3. ....

TODAY .... I AM GRATEFUL FOR:

1. ....

2. ....

3. ....

TODAY .... I AM GRATEFUL FOR:

1. ....

2. ....

3. ....

TODAY .... I AM GRATEFUL FOR:

1. ....

2. ....

3. ....

TODAY .... I AM GRATEFUL FOR:

1. ....

2. ....

3. ....

This week ....

TODAY ....   I AM GRATEFUL FOR:

1. ....

2. ....

3. ....

TODAY ....   I AM GRATEFUL FOR:

1. ....

2. ....

3. ....

TODAY ....   I AM GRATEFUL FOR:

1. ....

2. ....

3. ....

TODAY .... I AM GRATEFUL FOR:

1. ....

2. ....

3. ....

TODAY .... I AM GRATEFUL FOR:

1. ....

2. ....

3. ....

TODAY .... I AM GRATEFUL FOR:

1. ....

2. ....

3. ....

TODAY .... I AM GRATEFUL FOR:

1. ....

2. ....

3. ....

This week ....

TODAY ....   I AM GRATEFUL FOR:

1. ....

2. ....

3. ....

TODAY ....   I AM GRATEFUL FOR:

1. ....

2. ....

3. ....

TODAY ....   I AM GRATEFUL FOR:

1. ....

2. ....

3. ....

TODAY .... I AM GRATEFUL FOR:

1. ....

2. ....

3. ....

TODAY .... I AM GRATEFUL FOR:

1. ....

2. ....

3. ....

TODAY .... I AM GRATEFUL FOR:

1. ....

2. ....

3. ....

TODAY .... I AM GRATEFUL FOR:

1. ....

2. ....

3. ....

This week ....

TODODAY ....   I AM GRATEFUL FOR:

1. ....

2. ....

3. ....

TODAY ....   I AM GRATEFUL FOR:

1. ....

2. ....

3. ....

TODAY ....   I AM GRATEFUL FOR:

1. ....

2. ....

3. ....

TODAY .... I AM GRATEFUL FOR:

1. ....

2. ....

3. ....

TODAY .... I AM GRATEFUL FOR:

1. ....

2. ....

3. ....

TODAY .... I AM GRATEFUL FOR:

1. ....

2. ....

3. ....

TODAY .... I AM GRATEFUL FOR:

1. ....

2. ....

3. ....

This week ....

TODEY ....   I AM GRATEFUL FOR:

1. ....

2. ....

3. ....

TODEY ....   I AM GRATEFUL FOR:

1. ....

2. ....

3. ....

TODEY ....   I AM GRATEFUL FOR:

1. ....

2. ....

3. ....

TODAY .... I AM GRATEFUL FOR:

1. ....

2. ....

3. ....

TODAY .... I AM GRATEFUL FOR:

1. ....

2. ....

3. ....

TODAY .... I AM GRATEFUL FOR:

1. ....

2. ....

3. ....

TODAY .... I AM GRATEFUL FOR:

1. ....

2. ....

3. ....

This week ....

TODAY .... I AM GRATEFUL FOR:

1. ....

2. ....

3. ....

TODAY .... I AM GRATEFUL FOR:

1. ....

2. ....

3. ....

TODAY .... I AM GRATEFUL FOR:

1. ....

2. ....

3. ....

TODAY .... I AM GRATEFUL FOR:

1. ....

2. ....

3. ....

TODAY .... I AM GRATEFUL FOR:

1. ....

2. ....

3. ....

TODAY .... I AM GRATEFUL FOR:

1. ....

2. ....

3. ....

TODAY .... I AM GRATEFUL FOR:

1. ....

2. ....

3. ....

This week ....

TODAY ....   I AM GRATEFUL FOR:

1. ....

2. ....

3. ....

TODAY ....   I AM GRATEFUL FOR:

1. ....

2. ....

3. ....

TODAY ....   I AM GRATEFUL FOR:

1. ....

2. ....

3. ....

TODAY .... I AM GRATEFUL FOR:

1. ....
2. ....
3. ....

TODAY .... I AM GRATEFUL FOR:

1. ....
2. ....
3. ....

TODAY .... I AM GRATEFUL FOR:

1. ....
2. ....
3. ....

TODAY .... I AM GRATEFUL FOR:

1. ....
2. ....
3. ....

This week ....

TODAY .... I AM GRATEFUL FOR:

1. ....
2. ....
3. ....

TODAY .... I AM GRATEFUL FOR:

1. ....
2. ....
3. ....

TODAY .... I AM GRATEFUL FOR:

1. ....
2. ....
3. ....

TODAY .... I AM GRATEFUL FOR:

1. ....
2. ....
3. ....

TODAY .... I AM GRATEFUL FOR:

1. ....
2. ....
3. ....

TODAY .... I AM GRATEFUL FOR:

1. ....
2. ....
3. ....

TODAY .... I AM GRATEFUL FOR:

1. ....
2. ....
3. ....

This week ....

TODAY .... I AM GRATEFUL FOR:

1. ....

2. ....

3. ....

TODAY .... I AM GRATEFUL FOR:

1. ....

2. ....

3. ....

TODAY .... I AM GRATEFUL FOR:

1. ....

2. ....

3. ....

TODAY .... I AM GRATEFUL FOR:

1. ....
2. ....
3. ....

TODAY .... I AM GRATEFUL FOR:

1. ....
2. ....
3. ....

TODAY .... I AM GRATEFUL FOR:

1. ....
2. ....
3. ....

TODAY .... I AM GRATEFUL FOR:

1. ....
2. ....
3. ....

This week ....

TODAY .... I AM GRATEFUL FOR:

1. ....

2. ....

3. ....

TODAY .... I AM GRATEFUL FOR:

1. ....

2. ....

3. ....

TODAY .... I AM GRATEFUL FOR:

1. ....

2. ....

3. ....

TODAY .... I AM GRATEFUL FOR:

1. ....

2. ....

3. ....

TODAY .... I AM GRATEFUL FOR:

1. ....

2. ....

3. ....

TODAY .... I AM GRATEFUL FOR:

1. ....

2. ....

3. ....

TODAY .... I AM GRATEFUL FOR:

1. ....

2. ....

3. ....

This week ....

TODODAY .... I AM GRATEFUL FOR:

1. ....

2. ....

3. ....

TODAY .... I AM GRATEFUL FOR:

1. ....

2. ....

3. ....

TODAY .... I AM GRATEFUL FOR:

1. ....

2. ....

3. ....

TODAY .... I AM GRATEFUL FOR:

1. ....

2. ....

3. ....

TODAY .... I AM GRATEFUL FOR:

1. ....

2. ....

3. ....

TODAY .... I AM GRATEFUL FOR:

1. ....

2. ....

3. ....

TODAY .... I AM GRATEFUL FOR:

1. ....

2. ....

3. ....

This week ....

TODAY ....   I AM GRATEFUL FOR:

1. ....

2. ....

3. ....

TODAY ....   I AM GRATEFUL FOR:

1. ....

2. ....

3. ....

TODAY ....   I AM GRATEFUL FOR:

1. ....

2. ....

3. ....

TODAY .... I AM GRATEFUL FOR:

1. ....

2. ....

3. ....

TODAY .... I AM GRATEFUL FOR:

1. ....

2. ....

3. ....

TODAY .... I AM GRATEFUL FOR:

1. ....

2. ....

3. ....

TODAY .... I AM GRATEFUL FOR:

1. ....

2. ....

3. ....

This week ....

TODAY .... I AM GRATEFUL FOR:

1. ....

2. ....

3. ....

TODAY .... I AM GRATEFUL FOR:

1. ....

2. ....

3. ....

TODAY .... I AM GRATEFUL FOR:

1. ....

2. ....

3. ....

TODAY .... I AM GRATEFUL FOR:

1. ....

2. ....

3. ....

TODAY .... I AM GRATEFUL FOR:

1. ....

2. ....

3. ....

TODAY .... I AM GRATEFUL FOR:

1. ....

2. ....

3. ....

TODAY .... I AM GRATEFUL FOR:

1. ....

2. ....

3. ....

This week ....

TODAY .... I AM GRATEFUL FOR:

1. ....

2. ....

3. ....

TODAY .... I AM GRATEFUL FOR:

1. ....

2. ....

3. ....

TODAY .... I AM GRATEFUL FOR:

1. ....

2. ....

3. ....

TODAY .... I AM GRATEFUL FOR:

1. ....

2. ....

3. ....

TODAY .... I AM GRATEFUL FOR:

1. ....

2. ....

3. ....

TODAY .... I AM GRATEFUL FOR:

1. ....

2. ....

3. ....

TODAY .... I AM GRATEFUL FOR:

1. ....

2. ....

3. ....

This week ....

TODAY ....   I AM GRATEFUL FOR:

1. ....
2. ....
3. ....

TODAY ....   I AM GRATEFUL FOR:

1. ....
2. ....
3. ....

TODAY ....   I AM GRATEFUL FOR:

1. ....
2. ....
3. ....

TODAY .... I AM GRATEFUL FOR:

1. ....

2. ....

3. ....

TODAY .... I AM GRATEFUL FOR:

1. ....

2. ....

3. ....

TODAY .... I AM GRATEFUL FOR:

1. ....

2. ....

3. ....

TODAY .... I AM GRATEFUL FOR:

1. ....

2. ....

3. ....

This week ....

TODAY ....   I AM GRATEFUL FOR:
1. ....
2. ....
3. ....

TODAY ....   I AM GRATEFUL FOR:
1. ....
2. ....
3. ....

TODAY ....   I AM GRATEFUL FOR:
1. ....
2. ....
3. ....

TODAY .... I AM GRATEFUL FOR:

1. ....

2. ....

3. ....

TODAY .... I AM GRATEFUL FOR:

1. ....

2. ....

3. ....

TODAY .... I AM GRATEFUL FOR:

1. ....

2. ....

3. ....

TODAY .... I AM GRATEFUL FOR:

1. ....

2. ....

3. ....

This week ....

TODODAY ....   I AM GRATEFUL FOR:

1. ....

2. ....

3. ....

TODODAY ....   I AM GRATEFUL FOR:

1. ....

2. ....

3. ....

TODODAY ....   I AM GRATEFUL FOR:

1. ....

2. ....

3. ....

TODAY .... I AM GRATEFUL FOR:

1. ....

2. ....

3. ....

TODAY .... I AM GRATEFUL FOR:

1. ....

2. ....

3. ....

TODAY .... I AM GRATEFUL FOR:

1. ....

2. ....

3. ....

TODAY .... I AM GRATEFUL FOR:

1. ....

2. ....

3. ....

This week ....

TODODAY .... I AM GRATEFUL FOR:

1. ....

2. ....

3. ....

TODAY .... I AM GRATEFUL FOR:

1. ....

2. ....

3. ....

TODAY .... I AM GRATEFUL FOR:

1. ....

2. ....

3. ....

TODAY .... I AM GRATEFUL FOR:

1. ....

2. ....

3. ....

TODAY .... I AM GRATEFUL FOR:

1. ....

2. ....

3. ....

TODAY .... I AM GRATEFUL FOR:

1. ....

2. ....

3. ....

TODAY .... I AM GRATEFUL FOR:

1. ....

2. ....

3. ....

This week ....

TODAY ....   I AM GRATEFUL FOR:

1. ....
2. ....
3. ....

TODAY ....   I AM GRATEFUL FOR:

1. ....
2. ....
3. ....

TODAY ....   I AM GRATEFUL FOR:

1. ....
2. ....
3. ....

TODAY .... I AM GRATEFUL FOR:

1. ....

2. ....

3. ....

TODAY .... I AM GRATEFUL FOR:

1. ....

2. ....

3. ....

TODAY .... I AM GRATEFUL FOR:

1. ....

2. ....

3. ....

TODAY .... I AM GRATEFUL FOR:

1. ....

2. ....

3. ....

This week ....

TODAY .... I AM GRATEFUL FOR:

1. ....

2. ....

3. ....

TODAY .... I AM GRATEFUL FOR:

1. ....

2. ....

3. ....

TODAY .... I AM GRATEFUL FOR:

1. ....

2. ....

3. ....

TODAY .... I AM GRATEFUL FOR:

1. ....

2. ....

3. ....

TODAY .... I AM GRATEFUL FOR:

1. ....

2. ....

3. ....

TODAY .... I AM GRATEFUL FOR:

1. ....

2. ....

3. ....

TODAY .... I AM GRATEFUL FOR:

1. ....

2. ....

3. ....

This week ....

TODAY ....   I AM GRATEFUL FOR:

1. ....

2. ....

3. ....

TODAY ....   I AM GRATEFUL FOR:

1. ....

2. ....

3. ....

TODAY ....   I AM GRATEFUL FOR:

1. ....

2. ....

3. ....

TODAY .... I AM GRATEFUL FOR:

1. ....

2. ....

3. ....

TODAY .... I AM GRATEFUL FOR:

1. ....

2. ....

3. ....

TODAY .... I AM GRATEFUL FOR:

1. ....

2. ....

3. ....

TODAY .... I AM GRATEFUL FOR:

1. ....

2. ....

3. ....

Made in the USA
Columbia, SC
22 June 2022